Contents

1 Introduction to Cloud Search

Cloud computing offers a transformative approach to information retrieval, fundamentally altering how we build and deploy search solutions. Unlike traditional on-premise systems, the cloud provides scalability, elasticity, and cost-effectiveness, crucial for handling the ever-growing volume and variety of data. Understanding the foundational cloud models, Infrastructure as a Service (IaaS) and Software as a Service (SaaS), is paramount. IaaS provides you with the raw computing resources, letting you manage the infrastructure yourself, giving you complete control but requiring significant expertise. Conversely, SaaS offers fully managed search services, simplifying deployment but limiting customization options. The choice between these models depends heavily on your technical expertise, budget, and specific requirements. Selecting the right model greatly impacts your project's success and cost efficiency.
Moving beyond the infrastructure, let's consider the diverse search paradigms available in the cloud. Keyword-based search, the most prevalent approach, relies on matching user-entered keywords with indexed terms within documents. While simple to implement, it often lacks the nuance to understand the semantic meaning of queries. Semantic search, an increasingly popular alternative, employs natural language processing (NLP) techniques to understand the intent

and context of queries, providing more relevant results. Faceted search allows users to refine their search using pre-defined filters, enabling highly targeted searches within massive datasets. The selection of an appropriate paradigm influences not only the complexity of your implementation but also its effectiveness in meeting user needs. Careful consideration at this stage ensures a tailored solution that accurately meets requirements.

The flexibility of cloud-based search extends to integrating with various data sources. This allows you to build unified search experiences that span across multiple platforms and systems. Imagine seamlessly integrating internal documents with public web data and social media feeds, all within a single search interface. This comprehensive approach requires careful planning and the utilization of appropriate connectors and APIs to effectively bridge various data sources. Mastering this aspect is pivotal for creating truly powerful and comprehensive search applications.

Deployment strategies greatly influence the performance and scalability of your cloud-based search solution. A well-architected solution uses a distributed indexing approach to efficiently handle large datasets, dividing them across multiple servers for parallel processing. Efficient query processing relies on optimizing search algorithms and using caching mechanisms to minimize response times. Intelligent data partitioning ensures optimal resource utilization by spreading data evenly across available resources, preventing bottlenecks and improving overall performance. These architectural decisions have a substantial impact on the overall responsiveness and stability of your application and are key factors to address for long term success.

Security considerations are paramount when dealing with sensitive data in the cloud. Implementing robust access control mechanisms is essential to restrict access to authorized users only, adhering to stringent security protocols. Data encryption ensures confidentiality, safeguarding sensitive information both in transit and at rest. Compliance with relevant regulations, such as GDPR and HIPAA, is crucial, demonstrating commitment to responsible data handling and user privacy. Neglecting these aspects can lead to significant legal and reputational risks, making it an important part of your planning. Building trust with your users is fundamental in the digital world, and security practices form a cornerstone for this trust.

Choosing the right cloud provider is a significant decision, impacting various aspects of your project. Factors like scalability, cost, security features, and the available support resources all play a crucial role. Each provider offers distinct advantages and disadvantages, and the optimal choice depends on the specific needs of your application. Thorough research and due diligence are critical in ensuring that your provider aligns perfectly with your project requirements, providing the ideal environment for optimal performance and scalability.

Finally, remember the iterative nature of building a cloud-based search solution. Continuous monitoring and performance analysis are crucial for optimizing your system. Regularly assessing key metrics like query latency, throughput, and resource utilization reveals opportunities for improvement and allows you to proactively address potential issues before they negatively affect the user experience. This proactive approach enhances not only performance, but also reflects a commitment to efficiency and cost-effectiveness. Continuous refinement is key to a successful and enduring solution.

1.1 Cloud Computing Fundamentals

Cloud computing offers a transformative approach to data storage and processing, fundamentally altering how we handle information. It's characterized by on-demand self-service, broad network access, resource pooling, rapid elasticity, and measured service. These attributes make it uniquely suited for the challenges of information retrieval in big data environments, particularly the need for scalability and flexibility. Understanding these core principles is vital before diving into specific search architectures.

Unlike traditional on-premise solutions, cloud computing provides access to vast computational resources without the upfront investment in hardware. This pay-as-you-go model significantly reduces capital expenditure and allows businesses to scale their infrastructure up or down based on their specific needs. Imagine needing to handle a sudden surge in search queries during a major marketing campaign - cloud computing effortlessly accommodates this, while a fixed infrastructure would struggle to keep up, potentially leading to significant service disruption. This dynamic scalability is a cornerstone of building robust and responsive search solutions.

Several service models exist within the cloud computing paradigm. Infrastructure as a Service (IaaS) provides the fundamental building blocks—virtual machines, storage, and networks—allowing you to build and manage your own search infrastructure from the ground up. Conversely, Platform as a Service (PaaS) offers a more abstracted environment, providing pre-configured platforms and tools to simplify development and deployment. Finally, Software as a Service (SaaS) delivers ready-to-use search applications, requiring minimal technical expertise. The optimal choice depends heavily on your technical resources, budget, and the complexity of your search requirements. Choosing wisely from the start can save significant time and money in the long run.

Consider the security implications carefully. While cloud providers invest heavily in security, you retain responsibility for protecting your data. Understanding the security features offered by your chosen provider—access controls, encryption, and compliance certifications—is paramount. Failure to implement appropriate security measures can lead to significant data breaches and reputational damage, ultimately undermining the benefits of adopting cloud computing. Integrating robust security practices into your cloud search architecture is not an optional extra; it's a foundational requirement.

Moreover, the geographical distribution of cloud resources offers opportunities for optimization. By strategically placing your data and search infrastructure closer to your users, you can significantly reduce latency and improve the responsiveness of your search application. This is particularly crucial for applications serving geographically dispersed user bases, ensuring a consistently smooth search experience regardless of location. A global deployment strategy allows you to distribute the workload efficiently across various regions, offering redundancy and resilience in case of outages. Optimizing geographical placement is a powerful tool for enhancing both performance and reliability.

The cost-effectiveness of cloud computing is not simply about avoiding upfront hardware costs. Efficient resource utilization is key. Cloud monitoring tools allow you to track resource consumption, identify bottlenecks, and optimize your infrastructure to minimize expenses without compromising performance. Proper monitoring also enables proactive identification and resolution of potential problems, preventing costly downtime. This continuous optimization is a key factor in maintaining both cost-efficiency and service availability over the long term. Without diligent monitoring, cloud costs can spiral out of control, potentially negating many of the advantages of cloud adoption. Careful planning and proactive management are essential.

Finally, remember the importance of vendor lock-in. Choosing a cloud provider is a significant decision with long-term implications. Carefully evaluate the provider's reputation, service level agreements, and the portability of your data and applications. Avoiding vendor lock-in ensures flexibility and prevents being tied to a specific provider, allowing for easier migration or integration with other services in the future should your needs change. This strategic foresight is crucial for maintaining the adaptability of your search solution over its lifetime. Choosing a provider with a robust API and open standards is a key factor in minimizing future risks.

1.2 Search Paradigms

Understanding search paradigms is fundamental to building effective cloud-based search solutions. Different approaches cater to distinct needs and data structures, impacting the overall architecture and performance. Choosing the right paradigm is crucial in the early stages of development, shaping decisions on indexing, query processing, and data storage. A poorly chosen paradigm can lead to significant challenges later in the development cycle, potentially resulting in costly rework and suboptimal performance.

Keyword-based search remains a dominant paradigm, especially for simple, text-heavy data. This approach relies on matching keywords within documents to user queries, often using techniques like inverted indexing for efficiency. Its simplicity and speed are attractive, making it suitable for applications with straightforward search needs and well-defined keywords. However, keyword-based search often struggles with semantic nuances, synonyms, and variations in language, leading to incomplete or irrelevant results.

Semantic search aims to overcome these limitations by understanding the meaning and context of queries and documents. Instead of relying solely on keyword matches, semantic search utilizes techniques like natural language processing (NLP) and vector space models to identify relationships between words and concepts. This approach delivers more relevant results, even if the exact keywords are not present in the documents. The increased complexity, however, introduces computational overhead and necessitates more sophisticated indexing and query processing techniques.

Faceted search enhances the user experience by enabling more refined searches through filtering and categorization. Users can progressively refine their search results by selecting specific facets or attributes. Think of filtering e-commerce results by price range, color, or brand. This paradigm is particularly effective when dealing with structured data or when users need granular control over their search results. While powerful, successful implementation of faceted search requires careful design of the facets themselves and a robust indexing strategy to handle the various filtering combinations.

Hybrid approaches frequently combine elements of keyword-based, semantic, and faceted search to leverage their strengths. For instance, a system could initially employ keyword-based search for speed, followed by semantic search to refine results and finally, faceted search to allow user filtering. This strategy balances the need for speed and accuracy with the desire for a rich user interface. The design complexities increase with the hybrid approach, demanding careful integration and management of multiple components.

In selecting a paradigm, factors like data volume, data structure, query complexity, and user needs must be thoroughly considered. A simple keyword-based system might suffice for smaller datasets with straightforward queries. However, larger datasets with complex queries and nuanced semantic relationships necessitate more advanced paradigms like semantic search. The choice is not always clear-cut and requires a careful analysis of the specific requirements and constraints of the application. Remember that the chosen paradigm will significantly influence the architecture, technologies, and resources required for your cloud-based search solution. Therefore, investing the necessary time in selecting the optimal search paradigm is crucial for long-term success. A well-defined strategy ensures efficiency, scalability, and a superior user experience. Ignoring these considerations can lead to a search system that struggles to meet the evolving needs of its users. This careful consideration pays dividends in the form of a more efficient, user-friendly, and ultimately, successful search solution. The flexibility and scalability of cloud environments enable experimentation and adaptation, allowing for shifts in search paradigms as your needs evolve. Continuously assess and re-evaluate your approach, remaining prepared to adapt to changing data characteristics and user behaviors. The dynamic nature of cloud computing lends itself to this iterative approach, encouraging ongoing optimization and improvement. This adaptable approach is a key advantage in leveraging cloud-based technologies for information retrieval.

2 Designing Scalable Architectures

Designing efficient query processing is paramount for a scalable search architecture. Simply put, you need your system to handle a huge number of searches concurrently without significant delays. This involves optimizing various aspects of the query pipeline, from parsing and analyzing the query itself to retrieving and ranking the relevant documents. Consider using techniques like query rewriting to improve precision, or techniques such as distributed query processing across multiple nodes to handle the workload effectively, distributing the task among multiple servers and improving response times drastically. Furthermore, caching frequently accessed data is a highly effective strategy to reduce latency, essentially storing the results of frequently executed queries. This way the system doesn't have to perform the complex process repeatedly; instead, it can quickly retrieve results from the cache. The importance of caching cannot be overstated in enhancing the speed and responsiveness of your search system. Efficient query processing is a critical element of providing a satisfying user experience; a slow search engine is a frustrating one.

Effective data partitioning is a cornerstone of scalability. Imagine trying to search a single, massive database - it would be incredibly slow. Data partitioning strategically divides your data into smaller, manageable chunks, distributed across multiple servers. This approach significantly reduces the load on any individual server, enhancing performance. Several strategies exist, including range partitioning, hash partitioning, and list partitioning. Choosing the optimal method depends heavily on the nature of your data and query patterns. Range partitioning, for instance, is ideal when your data has a natural ordering (like dates). Hash partitioning, on the other hand, distributes data evenly across servers, minimizing imbalances. Careful consideration of your data and expected queries is essential for selecting the most efficient partitioning strategy; otherwise, performance gains will be limited, and inefficiencies will arise.

Distributed indexing is crucial for handling massive datasets. A single index server would quickly become overwhelmed by the sheer volume of data in a large-scale search system. Instead, a distributed index divides the indexing task among multiple servers, each responsible for a portion of the overall data. This parallel processing allows for significantly faster indexing speeds. However, ensuring consistency and synchronization across these distributed indexes is critical to maintain data integrity. To achieve this, it's important to implement robust mechanisms to handle updates and ensure all nodes reflect the most recent version of the index. This might involve using techniques such as consistent hashing or other strategies designed for distributed systems to manage data consistency and ensure all servers have the most updated information. Techniques like these are crucial for maintaining data integrity and reliability in a large-scale system.

Building a robust and scalable search system requires careful planning and design. Remember, scalability isn't just about handling more data; it's also about adapting to fluctuating user demand. Consider using load balancing techniques to distribute incoming requests efficiently across multiple servers. This will prevent any single server from becoming a bottleneck, improving overall system performance. Scaling your infrastructure to meet anticipated growth, both in data volume and user traffic is also crucial. This requires thoughtful consideration of your future needs and a clear path for scaling your system to accommodate those needs. Cloud infrastructure offers many advantages in this regard, providing the flexibility to scale resources up or down based on demand and even allowing you to choose the underlying hardware infrastructure. Thoroughly assess your present and future needs to design a system that can gracefully handle fluctuations in user load and data volume.

Consider horizontal scaling. In this model, you add more servers to handle the increasing load, spreading the workload across a larger pool of resources, rather than increasing the capabilities of an individual machine, which is vertical scaling. Horizontal scaling offers greater flexibility and scalability. It also offers fault tolerance, since the failure of one server doesn't necessarily bring down the whole system. The distributed nature of the system allows it to continue functioning even with some components offline. This redundancy is critical for ensuring high availability, a key aspect of building a robust and dependable system. Carefully consider how you'll manage these components, as the number of servers increases. Think about the tools you need to administer, monitor, and manage a large cluster of machines effectively.

Furthermore, efficient resource utilization is vital for cost-effectiveness. Monitoring CPU usage, memory consumption, and network I/O is crucial to identifying potential bottlenecks and optimizing resource allocation. This might involve adjusting server configurations, implementing caching strategies, or even migrating to more powerful hardware. Analyzing performance metrics will give you insights into where improvements are needed to fully utilize your resources. By understanding what your system is doing, you can take proactive steps to address inefficiencies and optimize your resource utilization. Through diligent monitoring and analysis, you can minimize waste and maximize the efficiency of your system, which will not only improve performance but also reduce operational costs. Continuously monitor and fine-tune to ensure efficient resource utilization. The ability to scale effectively is essential for the long-term success of your search solution. A well-designed architecture can handle future growth, providing a stable and reliable service for users.

2.1 Distributed Indexing

Effective distributed indexing is paramount for handling the massive datasets inherent in cloud-based search. Consider a scenario where your search index grows to terabytes, even petabytes, of data. A single machine simply can't cope. This necessitates distributing the index across multiple machines, allowing for parallel processing and improved scalability. The key is to maintain the illusion of a single, unified index to the end-user, despite the underlying distributed nature.

Efficient data partitioning is fundamental to this process. You wouldn't want to simply split the data randomly; instead, you need a strategy that minimizes data duplication and maximizes query efficiency. Hashing techniques, where documents are assigned to machines based on a hash function applied to a key field, are frequently used. This ensures relatively even distribution, but considerations such as data skew (where certain parts of the data are far larger than others) need careful management to prevent overloading specific machines. Range partitioning, where data is split into contiguous ranges based on a specific field like timestamp or ID, is another viable option, offering simpler query processing when the queries involve range comparisons.

Maintaining index consistency across distributed nodes is crucial. This requires a robust mechanism for managing updates and ensuring all nodes have a consistent view of the index. Replication is essential for fault tolerance; maintaining multiple copies of the index across different nodes ensures that if one node fails, the search service remains operational. Strategies such as master-slave replication, where updates are first written to a master node and then replicated to slave nodes, provide a straightforward approach. However, more sophisticated techniques like Paxos or Raft consensus protocols are necessary for maintaining consistency in the face of concurrent updates and network partitions. Choosing the right consistency model (strong vs. eventual consistency) is critical; it involves trading off consistency guarantees for performance and availability depending on your application's requirements.

In practice, managing a distributed index involves significant complexity. Efficient communication between nodes is paramount for managing updates, resolving conflicts, and routing queries. This typically requires a dedicated messaging system or a distributed coordination service, allowing nodes to seamlessly communicate and maintain a cohesive view of the data. Tools like Apache Kafka or Apache ZooKeeper are often deployed for this purpose, simplifying the coordination and management of these distributed components. Regular monitoring and logging of the index's health and performance are essential; this allows for early detection of problems like node failures, network issues, or data imbalances. Automated alerts and robust error handling mechanisms are vital for maintaining system reliability and ensuring continuous service.

Consider the indexing process itself. It isn't simply a matter of distributing data; it also involves distributing the workload of indexing new documents. This might involve using a distributed task queue, like Celery or RabbitMQ, to distribute indexing jobs across multiple worker nodes. This ensures that the indexing process scales efficiently with increasing data volume, preventing bottlenecks and ensuring that the system can handle the influx of new data without impacting search performance. Moreover, effective load balancing is crucial; it ensures that indexing workload is evenly distributed across all available machines, preventing overload on any single node.

Effective query routing is a crucial aspect. When a user submits a query, it must be efficiently directed to the appropriate nodes that hold the relevant data. A sophisticated query routing mechanism is needed. A centralized coordinator could route queries, but this could become a bottleneck. A more scalable solution would involve a decentralized approach where each node participates in routing queries based on its own knowledge of the data distribution. Consistent hashing techniques, combined with metadata about the data distribution on each node, are often employed in distributed query routing to minimize network hops and improve latency. Remember, the goal is to make the whole system seem seamless to the end-user, even though the search process might span many servers.

Finally, remember that building and maintaining a distributed index is an ongoing process. Regular maintenance, upgrades, and optimization are crucial to maintaining performance and scalability as your data grows and your system evolves. This includes techniques like rebalancing the data periodically to account for data skew, upgrading hardware as needed, and refining query processing strategies based on user behavior and performance monitoring data. Regular backups and disaster recovery procedures are also essential for mitigating risks associated with node failures or data loss. Choosing the right tools and technologies, and employing best practices, are key to building a robust and efficient distributed indexing solution.

2.2 Query Processing

Efficient query processing is the backbone of any scalable search solution. Without optimized query handling, even the most sophisticated indexing and data partitioning strategies will fail to deliver fast and relevant results. Consider a scenario with millions of documents; a poorly designed query process could lead to unacceptable delays, frustrating users and undermining the entire system's utility. This necessitates a deep understanding of efficient query strategies.
Optimizing query processing begins with understanding the query itself. Analyzing the query's structure, including the keywords, operators (AND, OR, NOT), and any proximity or phrase searches, is critical. This allows for the selection of the most appropriate search algorithm. For simple keyword searches, a straightforward inverted index lookup might suffice. More complex queries requiring semantic understanding might necessitate more sophisticated approaches like vector search utilizing techniques described in the "Advanced Indexing Techniques" chapter. The choice isn't arbitrary; it directly impacts performance and accuracy.
Furthermore, query optimization involves techniques like query rewriting and query expansion. Query rewriting can transform a poorly structured or ambiguous query into a more efficient form, yielding better results. For example, detecting spelling errors or

stemming words to their root form. Query expansion, on the other hand, enriches the query by adding related terms, improving recall—retrieving more relevant documents even if they don't contain the exact keywords specified. These techniques need careful implementation to avoid unintended consequences such as retrieving irrelevant results. The balance between precision and recall is a constant challenge in query optimization.

Efficient query processing necessitates leveraging the power of distributed systems. Distributing the query across multiple servers, especially relevant when dealing with massive datasets, ensures faster response times. This distribution is achieved through techniques like sharding, which involves dividing the index across multiple servers based on a chosen criterion (e.g., hash of the document ID). Careful planning of the sharding strategy is vital to avoid data skew and ensure even load distribution among servers, thereby preventing bottlenecks and maintaining consistent response times.

Caching is another crucial technique for improving query performance. Frequently accessed queries and their results can be stored in a cache, reducing the need to repeatedly perform expensive searches. Cache management strategies, including the replacement policy (e.g., Least Recently Used, or LRU) and cache invalidation mechanisms, influence cache efficiency. An effective caching strategy minimizes database load, considerably speeding up response times, especially for frequently repeated queries. However, poorly managed caching can lead to stale data and decreased accuracy.

Finally, monitoring and logging are crucial for understanding query performance and identifying areas for improvement. Collecting metrics such as query latency, throughput, and error rates helps pinpoint bottlenecks. Detailed logging provides insights into specific queries, revealing patterns and anomalies that might indicate problems with the query processing pipeline. This data-driven approach enables continuous optimization, ensuring the system remains efficient and responsive as data volume and user traffic increase. This aligns with the advice found in the "Monitoring and Optimization" chapter, applying those principles directly to the query processing component of the system. Remember, the goal is a seamless, efficient search experience for the end-user, a goal only achieved through proactive monitoring and continuous improvement in your query processing system.

2.3 Data Partitioning

Efficient data partitioning is crucial for building scalable and performant cloud-based search solutions. Poor partitioning can lead to significant performance bottlenecks, impacting query response times and overall system efficiency. Conversely, a well-designed partitioning strategy can dramatically improve search performance and scalability, enabling your system to handle massive datasets and high user traffic. The goal is to distribute the data evenly across your cluster, minimizing the load on any single node.

Choosing the right partitioning strategy depends heavily on your specific data characteristics and query patterns. Consider the size of your dataset, the frequency of updates, and the types of queries your users typically perform. For example, if your data is primarily textual and queries are primarily keyword-based, then a partitioning strategy based on the first letter of a document's title might be a reasonable approach. However, this would fall apart with a broader range of queries and data types. Imagine a system trying to handle multimedia data, or one designed to handle complex faceted searches \item simpler partitioning methods would fail dramatically.

Range partitioning is a common technique where data is divided into ranges based on a specific attribute. For instance, you might partition your data by date, assigning a range of dates to each partition. This works well when queries frequently filter by that attribute; for example, finding all documents created in a specific month. However, range partitioning becomes less efficient if your data distribution is uneven. If a large portion of your data falls within a single range, that partition will become a bottleneck, negating the scalability benefits. This is why careful consideration of your data distribution is so vital. Overlooking data skew can invalidate the effectiveness of any partitioning strategy.

Hash partitioning is another popular method, especially in scenarios where data distribution is unpredictable or uneven. A hash function maps each data item to a partition ID, distributing the data seemingly randomly. This generally leads to a more even distribution across partitions, mitigating the risk of hotspots. It's incredibly robust but requires a thorough understanding of hash functions and their properties to avoid collisions and ensure uniform distribution. This might require adjustments over time to accommodate changes in the overall data structure and distribution.

Composite partitioning combines multiple attributes to determine the partition assignment. This approach is particularly beneficial when queries often involve multiple filter criteria. For example, you might partition your data based on both a date range and a geographical location, allowing efficient processing of queries that filter by both time and place. It offers more fine-grained control, but increases the complexity of implementation and requires careful consideration of the attributes used for partitioning and their relative importance in search queries. The best strategy is not always intuitively obvious, and often requires considerable experimentation to achieve the optimal balance between efficiency and complexity. Regardless of your chosen method, efficient data partitioning requires regular monitoring and optimization. Track partition sizes, query response times, and resource utilization to identify potential bottlenecks and adjust your strategy as needed. Data distribution changes over time, and your initial partitioning scheme may become inefficient as your dataset grows or query patterns evolve. Dynamic partitioning strategies, allowing automated adjustments based on real-time data characteristics, can be immensely beneficial in maintaining optimal performance. This requires a system capable of monitoring load, detecting potential bottlenecks, and dynamically re-balancing partitions to counteract data skew, ensuring that your system continues to scale effectively. Ignoring this aspect can lead to unforeseen problems down the road, negating many of the initial benefits of meticulous planning.

Finally, remember that data partitioning is just one aspect of building a scalable search solution. It needs to work in concert with your choice of NoSQL database, indexing techniques, and query processing strategies. A well-designed, holistic architecture that considers all these factors is key to achieving the desired level of performance and scalability in your cloud-based search system. Therefore, the most effective strategy is always context-specific, and only careful consideration of the overall system architecture and query profiles can guarantee an optimal and robust search application. The choice of partitioning strategy should not be treated in isolation; it is inextricably linked to the wider architecture and ongoing performance monitoring.

3 NoSQL Databases for Search

Document databases, like MongoDB or Couchbase, excel at handling unstructured or semi-structured data, a common characteristic of search indices. Their flexible schema allows for easy adaptation as your data evolves. Imagine building a product search engine; you might need to add new fields for product attributes like color or size without major schema migrations, something crucial for agility in a rapidly changing market. This adaptability proves invaluable when dealing with the unpredictable nature of real-world data. The document-centric nature also makes it intuitive to store and retrieve rich, complex information, enhancing the richness of your search results. Efficient querying mechanisms further streamline your search processes. Therefore, leveraging document databases effectively contributes to building robust, scalable and easily maintainable search applications.

Graph databases, such as Neo4j or Amazon Neptune, shine when dealing with interconnected data. Consider a social media search application: finding people based on their connections or relationships becomes significantly more efficient. Graph databases excel at representing these relationships, allowing for complex queries that traverse the network of connections to retrieve relevant information. Their strength lies not just in storing data, but in swiftly exploring connections, a critical feature for relationship-based search queries. Unlike relational databases, which struggle with traversing complex relationships effectively, graph databases are optimized for this task. They offer a powerful tool for applications needing deep contextual understanding of data relationships, enriching the overall search experience.

Key-value stores, exemplified by Redis or Memcached, offer unparalleled speed for simple lookups. While not ideal for complex search queries, they are invaluable for caching frequently accessed data, significantly speeding up response times. Think of search suggestions: auto-completion features benefit greatly from the blazing speed of key-value stores, providing almost instantaneous feedback to users. This speed improvement directly enhances the user experience and contributes to a more responsive and satisfying search interaction. By strategically utilizing key-value stores for caching, you can dramatically improve the performance of your overall search system without significant architectural changes.

Wide-column stores, such as Cassandra or HBase, are designed for massive scalability and high availability. Imagine a large-scale e-commerce platform, handling millions of queries every second. The distributed nature of wide-column stores ensures the system can handle these demands without performance degradation. Their horizontal scalability permits easy expansion to accommodate increasing data volumes and user traffic, a vital aspect for continuously growing search applications. Their ability to handle large volumes of unstructured data, combined with efficient read/write operations, makes them an ideal choice for high-throughput search scenarios. The flexibility in schema and data modelling makes them versatile for various search applications.

Choosing the right database depends heavily on your specific requirements. The nature of your data (structured, semi-structured, or unstructured), the types of queries you anticipate, the required scalability, and performance demands all play crucial roles in this decision. A social network might benefit from a graph database's relationship-handling capabilities, whereas an e-commerce platform might prefer the scalability of a wide-column store. A blog search might perfectly suit a document database. Careful consideration of these factors is essential for building a search system that meets your specific needs and provides an optimal user experience. Consider factors like cost, ease of management, and the available expertise within your team when making your choice; this holistic approach guarantees a successful implementation. The initial investment in carefully selecting the right database can prevent costly migrations and rework down the line.

3.1 Document Stores

Document stores excel at handling semi-structured and unstructured data, making them ideal for search applications where the data doesn't neatly fit into relational tables. Think of documents like JSON or XML, or even plain text files; these are all easily managed within a document store. Their flexibility allows for schema-less designs, meaning you don't need to rigidly define data structures upfront, which is a significant advantage when dealing with evolving data formats or unpredictable content, especially prevalent in handling various user-generated content. This adaptability is crucial in dynamic environments. The ease of updating and modifying individual documents without impacting the entire database contributes to efficiency and maintainability.

Unlike relational databases, document stores offer scalability that's more easily adapted to changing demands. Horizontal scaling, adding more servers to handle increased load, is straightforward and often requires minimal code changes. This contrasts sharply with the complexity sometimes associated with scaling relational database systems, where schema changes and data distribution can be problematic. For applications expecting significant growth, this horizontal scalability is a game-changer. Choosing a horizontally scalable solution provides robustness and anticipates future growth with relative ease. This means less downtime and more consistent performance.

Consider the performance benefits. Document stores are optimized for retrieving specific documents based on unique identifiers or targeted queries. This means fetching individual items, or sets of closely related items, is exceptionally fast. This speed is particularly critical when dealing with large datasets where every millisecond counts for delivering a good user experience, especially for interactive applications. The speed increase translates directly into improved user satisfaction and engagement. This fast retrieval isn't simply about speed for its own sake; it supports a better user experience.

However, document stores aren't a silver bullet. Complex joins, the kind frequently employed in relational databases, are not their strength. If your search requirements involve intricately linking data across numerous documents based on multiple related fields, you may find document stores less effective. Relational databases handle such relationships much more efficiently. Carefully assess your needs; if relationships form the core of your data structure and your queries, a relational database might be a better fit. Mismatching your database to your data structure can lead to performance bottlenecks and operational difficulties.

Efficient querying is essential. While document stores don't support SQL directly, most provide query languages, such as MongoDB's query language, or other variations of specialized query capabilities using JSON structures and query expressions. These languages typically allow for flexible filtering and sorting based on document content, leveraging indexes for efficient searches. Understanding the query language specific to your chosen document store is crucial for optimal performance. Familiarize yourself with query optimization techniques to avoid slow and ineffective queries that severely impact performance.

Data modeling plays a pivotal role. Though schema-less, effective data modeling remains paramount. You still need to organize your data logically within documents, ensuring fields are properly named and structured for efficient querying and retrieval. Consistent naming conventions and well-defined data structures, even within a schema-less environment, significantly impact query performance and data integrity. Investing time in careful modeling avoids future maintenance headaches and performance issues. A well-defined data structure pays dividends in long-term maintainability.

Another critical aspect to consider is indexing. Document stores usually provide indexing capabilities, allowing you to optimize query performance by indexing frequently queried fields. Indexes significantly improve retrieval speed, just like in relational databases. Knowing which fields to index and how to manage indexes efficiently is vital for performance tuning. Over-indexing can lead to performance overhead, so it requires a balanced approach based on query patterns. Proper indexing reduces query times considerably.

Finally, when considering document stores, remember to factor in the vendor's ecosystem. Choose a vendor with a robust and well-documented API, strong community support, and a proven track record of reliability and scalability. The availability of tools and resources directly impacts your productivity and ability to solve problems quickly. Don't underestimate the value of a strong community; a large, active community provides invaluable support and resources. Look for a vendor and solution that offers the tools and support necessary for continued success and easier troubleshooting.

3.2 Graph Databases

Graph databases offer a powerful alternative to traditional relational databases when dealing with interconnected data, a common scenario in many large-scale search applications. Unlike relational databases that store data in tables with rows and columns, graph databases represent data as nodes and edges, mirroring the relationships between different pieces of information. This fundamentally different approach allows for efficient traversal and querying of complex relationships, crucial for tasks like recommendation engines, social network analysis, and knowledge graph searches. Their inherent flexibility in handling evolving data structures makes them particularly well-suited for dynamic environments typical of cloud-based systems.

Consider a scenario where you're building a search engine for a large e-commerce platform. Products are connected to categories, brands, and customer reviews. Relational databases would require multiple joins to retrieve information spanning these connections, often leading to performance bottlenecks, especially with massive datasets. A graph database, however, directly represents these relationships as edges between nodes. Retrieving all products related to a specific brand, including customer reviews, becomes a significantly faster and more efficient operation. This speed advantage is a direct consequence of the database's inherent structure, optimally designed for traversing relationships.

The inherent flexibility of graph databases allows for the easy addition of new types of connections and data points, accommodating the ever-evolving nature of online businesses and their vast quantities of data. Imagine adding a new feature, say, showing similar products based on customer purchase history. Adding this functionality to a relational database may necessitate schema modifications and significant code changes. With a graph database, you simply add new edges reflecting the purchase relationships, and the database readily adapts. This adaptability minimizes downtime and allows for quicker integration of new features, a crucial factor for remaining competitive in today's dynamic market.

Another key advantage is the ability to perform complex queries that explore multiple levels of relationships. Think about finding all products recommended to users who purchased a specific item and also viewed similar products in the past. This kind of multi-hop query can be incredibly complex in relational databases, resulting in convoluted SQL statements and potentially poor performance. Graph databases, however, excel at these kinds of queries, making the implementation simpler and significantly faster. This makes them ideal for implementing personalized recommendations or advanced search functionalities dependent on intricate relationships between data points.

However, graph databases aren't without their limitations. While excellent for managing relationships, they may not be the optimal choice for applications requiring complex analytical queries or high-volume transactional operations. Relational databases, with their structured schema and established query languages like SQL, often offer better performance in these areas. The key is understanding the specific needs of your search application and choosing the database technology that best aligns with those requirements. Properly evaluating the trade-offs between performance, scalability, and flexibility is critical for long-term success.

Implementing a graph database within a cloud-based search architecture presents specific considerations. Scalability is paramount, and choosing a graph database solution designed for distributed environments is essential. Cloud providers offer managed graph database services, simplifying deployment and maintenance, providing automatic scaling capabilities to handle fluctuating loads. These services often integrate seamlessly with other cloud services, such as storage and compute resources, simplifying the overall architecture. This integration can greatly streamline the development process and reduce the operational overhead.

Data modeling is another important aspect. Designing an effective graph schema that accurately represents the relationships in your data is crucial for optimal query performance. Understanding the trade-offs between schema complexity and query efficiency is paramount. Careful consideration must be given to node and edge properties, ensuring that the chosen model effectively captures the relevant relationships without introducing unnecessary complexity that hinders performance. Choosing the right model can significantly improve the efficiency of your search application.

Finally, choosing the right graph database technology depends on several factors including the scale of your data, the complexity of your queries, and your existing infrastructure. Several popular graph database solutions are available, each with its own strengths and weaknesses. Careful evaluation is necessary to identify the technology best suited to the specific needs of your cloud-based search application. A thorough understanding of these various options will greatly assist in making a suitable selection for a robust and scalable solution. Remember that selecting the appropriate technology is a vital step in creating a highly effective and well-performing system.

3.3 Key-Value Stores

Key-value stores, a foundational NoSQL database type, offer a straightforward approach to data storage, perfectly suited for certain aspects of large-scale search. Their simplicity, however, belies a surprising versatility when intelligently applied within a broader search architecture. Understanding their strengths and limitations is crucial for effectively leveraging them in your cloud-based search solution.

Unlike relational databases that organize data into tables with interconnected rows and columns, key-value stores maintain a simpler structure. Each data item consists of a unique key and its associated value. The key acts as an identifier, allowing for rapid retrieval of the corresponding value. This fundamental design contributes to their exceptional speed and scalability, particularly for read-heavy workloads. Think of it like a highly efficient dictionary where you can instantly look up a word (the key) and find its definition (the value).

The speed and simplicity of key-value stores make them ideal for caching frequently accessed data. In a search system, this translates to dramatically improved response times. For instance, you could cache popular search results or metadata associated with frequently queried documents. This reduces the load on your primary data sources and minimizes latency for users. Efficient caching significantly improves the user experience and overall system responsiveness, providing a faster, more seamless search experience. By strategically incorporating key-value caching, you can significantly enhance the performance and responsiveness of your search application. This approach allows for rapid retrieval of frequently accessed data, leading to improved query response times and a better user experience.

However, their simplicity also presents limitations. Complex queries involving relationships between data points are inefficient. You won't find the join capabilities of a relational database here. Instead, relationships must be managed through your application logic or by leveraging other database technologies in tandem with the key-value store. This architecture might necessitate additional processing steps to reconstruct data relationships and generate comprehensive search results. The need for application-level joins or auxiliary databases adds complexity and might affect overall performance.

Furthermore, key-value stores aren't ideally suited for complex data structures or schema enforcement. Relational databases impose structure through schemas, providing data integrity and consistency. Key-value stores offer flexibility but require more careful management of data formats to ensure consistency within your application. This necessitates careful planning and robust data validation mechanisms within the application to mitigate potential issues arising from data inconsistency. Inconsistency can affect the search results' accuracy and reliability, so rigorous validation is essential.

Despite these limitations, key-value stores can significantly benefit a cloud-based search architecture, particularly as a supporting component. They excel as a caching layer, augmenting the performance of other databases and providing swift access to frequently accessed data. They are also well suited for indexing data that can be easily represented in a key-value format, such as term frequencies within a document or metadata associated with specific documents. Careful planning and design are critical to successfully integrate key-value stores into your overall search system. Understanding their strengths, leveraging their efficiency for caching and simple indexing tasks, and compensating for their limitations through careful design choices is crucial for optimizing your system's performance and scalability. Remember to always consider the specific needs of your search application when deciding whether to incorporate key-value stores into your architecture. Their role, while supporting, can be critical to the overall efficiency and performance of your cloud-based search system. Used thoughtfully, key-value stores can become an invaluable asset. The proper integration of these components requires a thorough understanding of the strengths and limitations of each technology.

3.4 Wide-Column Stores

Wide-column stores, a type of NoSQL database, offer a compelling solution for specific search challenges in large-scale cloud environments. Their unique structure, designed around columns rather than rows, makes them particularly adept at handling data with high cardinality—meaning many different values for a single attribute. Imagine a scenario involving millions of product listings, each with numerous attributes like price, color, size, and manufacturer. Traditional relational databases would struggle with such extensive attribute variations, leading to performance bottlenecks and query inefficiencies. Wide-column stores, however, excel in this context because they allow flexible schema design and efficient querying across a specific subset of attributes.

The core strength of wide-column stores lies in their ability to store and retrieve large amounts of sparse data rapidly. This means data where many values are null or absent for each row. Unlike relational databases that enforce a rigid schema, requiring all columns to be present for every row, wide-column stores embrace sparsity. This efficiency stems from their column-family organization. Data is grouped into column families, which are essentially logical containers for related attributes. When querying, you only retrieve the necessary column families, avoiding the overhead of fetching irrelevant data. This attribute-based querying becomes significantly more efficient than row-based scans in scenarios with numerous, sparsely populated attributes.

Consider a typical e-commerce application. You might have a column family for product details (name, description, images), another for pricing information (price, discounts, currency), and yet another for inventory (stock levels, warehouse locations). This organizational structure allows for highly targeted queries. For instance, fetching the prices of all red shoes requires accessing only the relevant column families, ignoring all other product data. This selective retrieval drastically reduces the data volume processed and improves query response times—a crucial element for a positive user experience.

However, wide-column stores aren't a one-size-fits-all solution. Their architecture presents trade-offs. Joining data across multiple column families can be more complex and less efficient than joins in relational databases. Furthermore, transactions spanning multiple column families may be harder to implement reliably. These considerations are crucial for careful database selection. A deep understanding of your application's data access patterns and query requirements is essential for determining whether a wide-column store aligns with your needs.

Choosing the right database hinges on a thorough assessment of your specific requirements. If your application involves frequent querying of specific attributes across a large dataset with high cardinality, then a wide-column store may offer significant performance advantages. Its ability to handle sparse data effectively and enable targeted queries makes it a powerful option for scenarios such as user activity tracking, sensor data analysis, or time-series data management.

Yet, the flexibility and scalability of wide-column stores come at a cost. The absence of complex join operations might restrict certain types of analytical queries. Moreover, complex transactions might necessitate careful design and implementation to ensure data consistency and integrity. The lack of standardized query language also requires developers to learn a new querying paradigm, often specific to the chosen wide-column store implementation. Before committing to a wide-column store, it's crucial to understand the limitations and ensure they don't hinder your application's functionality. Carefully evaluate your data access patterns, querying needs, and the potential complexities of cross-column-family operations before making your decision.

In practice, many search applications benefit from a hybrid approach, combining the strengths of different database technologies. For example, you might use a wide-column store for storing and retrieving large amounts of indexed data and a relational database for managing structured metadata or user profiles. This layered architecture allows leveraging the best features of each database type, optimizing performance and scalability while ensuring data integrity. A well-designed hybrid system can adapt to the unique requirements of the application, maximizing efficiency and functionality.

Successfully implementing a wide-column store involves more than just choosing the right database; it requires careful planning and execution. Data modeling is crucial. You need to carefully design your column families and consider how data will be accessed and queried. Efficient data distribution strategies are also essential to avoid performance bottlenecks and ensure scalability. And finally, careful performance monitoring and tuning are needed to keep your database running efficiently and optimally under varying loads. This comprehensive approach will ensure that your wide-column store solution meets your needs and provides the desired performance and scalability. Remember, it's always best practice to extensively test and benchmark your solution before deployment to ensure it scales appropriately and meets your performance expectations.

3.5 Choosing the Right Database

Choosing the right database is crucial for building a successful cloud-based search system. The wrong choice can lead to performance bottlenecks, scalability issues, and ultimately, a poor user experience. Your choice depends heavily on the specific needs of your application, considering factors like data volume, data structure, query patterns, and scalability requirements.

For applications involving unstructured data like text and documents, document stores like MongoDB or Elasticsearch are excellent options. Their flexible schema allows for easy handling of diverse data formats, making them ideal for storing and searching textual content. Elasticsearch, in particular, offers powerful search capabilities built-in, including full-text search, faceting, and geospatial search. MongoDB, on the other hand, provides a more general-purpose document database solution, which might be preferred if your application needs extend beyond search functionality. Carefully consider the specific features each offers to ensure the best fit for your needs.

If your data has a strong relational structure, a relational database like PostgreSQL or MySQL might be a more suitable choice. While they might not offer the same level of scalability as some NoSQL options out of the box, they provide ACID properties (Atomicity, Consistency, Isolation, Durability), crucial for maintaining data integrity in transactional applications. However, for truly massive datasets, scaling relational databases can become complex and expensive, often requiring specialized techniques like sharding and replication. Thorough evaluation of data relationships and transaction requirements is key here.

For applications requiring complex relationships between data points, graph databases like Neo4j offer unique advantages. Their ability to efficiently traverse and query relationships makes them ideal for applications like social networks, recommendation engines, or knowledge graphs. Consider a graph database when your data is best represented as nodes and edges, allowing for quick identification of connections and relationships. The performance benefits in such scenarios often outweigh any potential complexities in managing a graph database.

Key-value stores, such as Redis or Memcached, are excellent for caching frequently accessed data. They offer extremely fast read and write speeds, ideal for improving the performance of your search application by storing frequently queried data in memory. Remember they are generally not suitable for persistent storage of your main search index; rather, they are best used as a supplementary layer to improve overall response times. Effective use requires a careful understanding of caching strategies and data eviction policies.

Wide-column stores, such as Cassandra or HBase, are designed for handling massive datasets with high write throughput. They excel at managing large volumes of structured and semi-structured data, making them suitable for applications requiring high availability and scalability. They're particularly well-suited for scenarios with high write loads and less stringent consistency requirements. However, their query flexibility is often less than that of document stores, so consider your query patterns carefully.

Ultimately, the best database for your cloud-based search system depends on a careful evaluation of several factors. Start by thoroughly analyzing the nature of your data, the types of queries you expect, your scalability needs, and the level of data integrity required. Consider the trade-offs between flexibility, scalability, and consistency when making your decision. Don't rush the process; choosing wisely is a significant factor in the long-term success of your project. Remember that prototyping with smaller datasets can help inform your choice and validate your architecture before committing to a full-scale deployment. A well-chosen database forms a crucial foundation for a high-performing and scalable cloud search solution. Choosing poorly can create significant future challenges and necessitate costly redesigns. Therefore, the preliminary stage of database selection demands thorough analysis and careful consideration. The right database lays the groundwork for efficient and effective search, forming a cornerstone of your system's overall success.

4 Advanced Indexing Techniques

Inverted indexes are the workhorses of many modern search engines. They're fundamentally efficient because they pre-compute the locations of every word within a document collection. This allows for incredibly fast lookups when a user submits a search query. Imagine trying to find all documents containing "quantum computing"—without an inverted index, you'd need to scan every single document, one by one. An inverted index, however, lets you instantly pinpoint documents containing that term, significantly reducing search time. This is crucial for handling the massive datasets typical in cloud-based search environments. Think of the sheer scale of data involved in indexing the entire web; inverted indexes are essential for keeping search responses snappy. The structure itself involves creating a dictionary of terms and then, for each term, a list of documents containing that term along with the specific locations of the term within each document. Adding positional information allows for more complex searches such as phrase searches. Efficient implementations of inverted indexes rely on careful data structure choices, like utilizing efficient data structures in memory to minimize access times during search queries. This aspect is particularly relevant for cloud environments where resource optimization is paramount.

Vector space models offer a fascinating alternative, especially when dealing with semantic search. Unlike keyword-based searches, which only focus on exact word matches, vector space models represent both documents and queries as vectors in a high-dimensional space. Each dimension represents a different term or concept, and the value in that dimension represents the importance of that term or concept within the document or query. This allows for the retrieval of documents that are semantically similar to the query, even if they don't share exact keywords. Imagine searching for "best Italian restaurants near me." A vector space model might retrieve restaurants even if their menu descriptions don't explicitly include those words. The model's ability to understand the context and related concepts—Italian cuisine, location proximity, quality ratings—makes it far more versatile than a simple keyword search. This semantic understanding is particularly relevant in domains like e-commerce, where users' queries are often less precise.

The construction of vector space models involves processes like term frequency-inverse document frequency (TF-IDF) calculations, which weigh the importance of terms based on how frequently they appear within a specific document and across the entire document collection. This method allows the system to prioritize terms that are significant within a particular document but less frequent across all documents, thus emphasizing uniqueness and relevance. Another crucial aspect involves choosing the appropriate dimensionality reduction techniques such as Principal Component Analysis (PCA) or Latent Semantic Analysis (LSA) to address the "curse of dimensionality" inherent in high-dimensional vector spaces, improving efficiency and accuracy. Effective dimensionality reduction techniques strike a balance between preserving the essential information within the vectors and reducing computational complexity. Therefore, the careful selection of these methods is vital for building efficient and accurate semantic search solutions.

While both inverted indexes and vector space models are powerful tools, they often complement each other. One effective strategy is using an inverted index for fast keyword retrieval, then refining the results using a vector space model to improve semantic relevance. This hybrid approach leverages the strengths of both methodologies—the speed of keyword-based indexing and the semantic understanding of vector space models—to deliver more accurate and satisfying search results. Consider a search engine for scientific papers. A keyword search could efficiently return papers containing certain terminology, but a vector space model could subsequently rank those papers based on their semantic similarity to the query, taking into account the context and relationships between concepts, resulting in a ranked list of highly relevant papers that are indeed very relevant to the user's purpose. This multi-pronged approach is particularly beneficial in complex domains with rich semantic relationships between concepts. Optimizing the interaction between these two methods is key to building truly advanced search solutions.

Finally, optimizing these advanced indexing techniques for a cloud environment involves careful consideration of resource allocation and distribution. The size of the index can be immense, so distributed indexing is often necessary. This means partitioning the index across multiple servers to handle the scale of data. Managing this distribution efficiently, balancing load across the servers, and ensuring data consistency is critical for maintaining the performance of the search engine. Cloud providers offer various managed services to simplify this process, but understanding the underlying principles is vital for making informed decisions about your architecture and for troubleshooting performance bottlenecks should they occur. Data replication strategies are also important to address high availability requirements, ensuring search functionality is not compromised in case of server failures. Effective monitoring and dynamic resource allocation are essential to ensuring the continued efficiency of your system as your dataset grows and your user base expands. A well-designed cloud-based search solution uses advanced indexing techniques not just for speed and accuracy, but also for scalability and resilience.

4.1 Inverted Indexes

Inverted indexes are the cornerstone of efficient keyword-based search. They represent a fundamental shift from the naive approach of linearly scanning every document for matching keywords, a strategy that becomes computationally crippling with large datasets. Instead, an inverted index maps each unique term (word or phrase) to a list of documents containing that term. This allows for incredibly fast retrieval, as the system only needs to consult the lists associated with the search terms, rather than examining the entire corpus.

Consider a simple example: a collection of three documents. Document 1 contains "cat dog bird"; Document 2 contains "dog bird"; and Document 3 contains "bird cat". A corresponding inverted index would structure the data as follows: "bird": [1, 2, 3], "cat": [1, 3], "dog": [1, 2]. Searching for "cat" instantly yields documents 1 and 3. The elegance and efficiency of this method become exponentially more apparent when dealing with millions or billions of documents and millions of terms.

However, building and maintaining such an index in a cloud environ-

ment presents unique challenges. Scalability is paramount. The index itself can become incredibly large, requiring distributed storage and processing. Furthermore, the constant influx of new documents necessitates efficient update mechanisms that minimize disruption to ongoing searches. Strategies like sharding, where the index is partitioned across multiple servers, are commonly employed to address these issues. Each shard manages a subset of terms and documents, enabling parallel processing and improving both query speed and the ability to handle large data volumes. Replication and redundancy are critical elements to ensure high availability and fault tolerance.
Furthermore, efficient data structures are vital. The choice of data structure profoundly impacts performance. While simple lists can suffice for small indexes, the use of more sophisticated structures like skip lists or B-trees becomes critical when dealing with millions of documents per term. These advanced structures allow for logarithmic time complexity in search operations, guaranteeing swift responses even under heavy load. Careful consideration must also be given to the indexing process itself. Techniques like stemming (reducing words to their root form) and stop word removal (filtering out common words like "the" and "a") can significantly reduce index size and improve search precision. These preprocessing steps are essential for optimizing performance.

The choice of the underlying storage system is also crucial for the effectiveness of an inverted index in a cloud setting. Distributed NoSQL databases, particularly those offering key-value or wide-column storage, often prove advantageous due to their inherent scalability and flexibility. The flexibility offered by such systems permits efficient handling of updates and modifications to the index, while the horizontal scalability ensures high availability and resilience. The decision regarding the most appropriate NoSQL database will depend on various factors like the volume of data, the frequency of updates, and the specific query patterns expected. This selection requires a careful evaluation of the trade-offs between different database features and their impact on search performance.

Moreover, maintaining the index is an ongoing process. Documents are constantly updated, added, or removed. Strategies for efficient incremental updates are essential to avoid creating the index from scratch each time changes occur. Techniques like log-structured merge-trees (LSM-trees) offer efficient handling of frequent updates. They allow for the asynchronous merging of updated index segments, ensuring that the search remains responsive while modifications are applied. This asynchronous approach is critical for maintaining a high level of responsiveness in the system. Moreover, the efficiency of updating the inverted index, whether it's incremental or complete rebuilds, is fundamental for maintaining the system's performance in the face of the ever-changing nature of data in a cloud-based system. Monitoring these update processes and adapting strategies as the system evolves is essential for long-term performance.

Finally, compression is a key factor in optimizing storage costs and improving query speed. Large inverted indexes can occupy substantial storage space; therefore, compression techniques like dictionary encoding or variable-length encoding are vital for efficiency. These compression schemes reduce the size of the index, leading to faster retrieval times and lower costs. The selection of a compression technique will depend on the specifics of the index and the trade-offs between compression ratio and the computational cost of encoding and decoding. Finding the optimal balance between the two is crucial for maintaining the cost-effectiveness and efficiency of the entire system. The constant evolution of compression technology necessitates ongoing evaluations of alternative approaches to keep the index optimized for both storage and query speed.

4.2 Vector Space Models

Vector space models offer a powerful alternative to traditional keyword-based search, enabling semantic understanding of text data. Unlike keyword matching, which relies on exact word occurrences, vector space models represent documents and queries as vectors in a high-dimensional space, where each dimension corresponds to a term or feature. The similarity between documents and queries is then calculated based on the proximity of their vectors. This allows the retrieval of documents semantically similar to the query, even if they don't share identical keywords.

Cosine similarity is a commonly used metric to measure the similarity between two vectors. It computes the cosine of the angle between the vectors, with a value of 1 indicating perfect similarity and 0 indicating no similarity. The calculation involves the dot product of the two vectors, divided by the product of their magnitudes. This approach effectively captures the directional relationship between the vectors, making it robust to differences in vector length. Efficient computation of cosine similarity on large datasets is crucial for practical applications, often requiring optimized algorithms and specialized hardware.

Constructing these vector representations involves several steps. First, a vocabulary of terms needs to be created from the corpus of documents. This can involve techniques like stemming and lemmatization to reduce words to their root forms. Next, each document is converted into a vector, where each element represents the weight of a term in the document. Various weighting schemes exist, such as TF-IDF (Term Frequency-Inverse Document Frequency), which considers both the frequency of a term within a document and its inverse frequency across the entire corpus. Higher TF-IDF values indicate more important terms for a given document.

The dimensionality of the vector space can be extremely high, especially with large corpora. Dimensionality reduction techniques, such as Latent Semantic Analysis (LSA) or Singular Value Decomposition (SVD), can significantly reduce computational costs and improve search accuracy by identifying latent semantic relationships between terms. These techniques effectively project the high-dimensional vectors into a lower-dimensional space while preserving important information. Careful consideration of the dimensionality reduction method and the appropriate number of dimensions is crucial for optimal performance.

Implementing vector space models requires careful selection of appropriate libraries and tools. Libraries like Gensim, spaCy, and scikit-learn provide powerful functionalities for text processing, vectorization, and similarity computation. They often integrate with cloud platforms like AWS or Google Cloud, facilitating the deployment of scalable search solutions. Consider the specific requirements of your application when choosing a library, focusing on factors like performance, scalability, and ease of integration with existing systems. Remember that proper data preprocessing, including cleaning, stemming, and stop word removal, is crucial for optimal results.

Scaling vector space models for large datasets presents unique challenges. The computational cost of calculating cosine similarity between a query vector and potentially millions of document vectors can be significant. Strategies like approximate nearest neighbor (ANN) search algorithms can alleviate this problem by efficiently retrieving documents close to the query vector without exhaustively comparing all documents. Techniques like Locality-Sensitive Hashing (LSH) and KD-trees are commonly used for ANN search. Choosing an appropriate ANN algorithm depends on several factors, including the dataset size, dimensionality, and desired accuracy. The trade-off between speed and accuracy should be carefully considered.

Beyond cosine similarity, other similarity metrics can be employed, offering different properties and potential advantages. For example, Jaccard similarity measures the overlap between the sets of terms in two documents. Other approaches, like Euclidean distance, can also be used, though they are less robust to differences in vector length. The choice of similarity metric should depend on the specific characteristics of the data and the desired search behavior. Experimentation and comparison of different metrics are often necessary to identify the optimal choice for a given application.

Furthermore, integrating vector space models with other search techniques can improve overall search effectiveness. For instance, combining vector space models with traditional keyword-based search can leverage the strengths of both approaches. This hybrid approach can provide a robust solution that captures both exact keyword matches and semantic similarities. Additionally, incorporating user feedback and clickstream data can enhance the relevance of search results over time, through techniques like learning to rank. This iterative refinement leads to a more personalized and effective search experience.

Finally, consider the limitations of vector space models. While they effectively capture semantic relationships, they may not perfectly reflect nuanced meanings or complex relationships between concepts. Additionally, the choice of vocabulary and weighting scheme significantly influences the results. Thorough evaluation and refinement of the model are crucial to ensure its accuracy and effectiveness for the specific application. Remember that a well-defined evaluation strategy, measuring precision, recall, and F1-score, is critical in assessing the performance of the vector space model.

5 Relevance Ranking and Scoring

Understanding how to rank search results is crucial for a successful cloud-based search system. We need to ensure the most relevant documents appear first, satisfying user queries and maximizing the effectiveness of your search solution. This chapter explores several key methods for achieving this, moving from simpler, established techniques to more sophisticated approaches utilizing machine learning.

TF-IDF, or Term Frequency-Inverse Document Frequency, is a foundational method. It works by assigning weights to words based on their frequency within a document and their rarity across the entire collection. Terms appearing frequently in a specific document but infrequently across the whole dataset receive a higher weight, indicating greater relevance. This simple yet powerful technique provides a baseline for ranking, easily implemented and understood, making it a great starting point for beginners. Consider, for instance, a search for "cloud computing security." Documents containing "cloud" and "security" frequently, but "computing" less frequently across your entire dataset, will be scored higher than those with just a single mention of each, highlighting the nuance TF-IDF offers. It's a cornerstone of many search engines.

PageRank, initially developed for ranking web pages, extends its relevance to cloud search. It operates on the principle of link analysis; a document's importance is inferred from the number and quality of links pointing to it. Adapting this to cloud search, you can interpret "links" as relationships between documents within your dataset. A document frequently referenced or linked to by other high-quality documents receives a higher PageRank score, suggesting greater relevance and authority. This indirect measure of importance is particularly valuable for establishing the authority of documents within a specific domain, effectively determining which documents are seen as more central and critical within the larger context of your collection. Implementing PageRank requires careful consideration of how to define and quantify these relationships within your data, making it a more complex but potentially rewarding approach.

Learning to Rank (LTR) represents a significant step up in complexity, yet offers greatly improved precision. Unlike the previous methods, LTR is a machine learning approach that uses training data - user interaction logs, for example - to learn optimal ranking functions. The system is fed examples of queries and their corresponding ranked results, then learns to predict ideal rankings for new queries. This personalized approach can adapt to changing user needs and provide far more fine-grained control over ranking. The implementation of LTR involves choosing an appropriate learning algorithm and carefully preparing your training data. This might seem daunting for beginners, but several readily available libraries and tools considerably simplify this process.

Consider a scenario where you have a large dataset of customer support articles. TF-IDF might rank articles based on keyword frequency, missing the context and user intent. PageRank could help highlight authoritative articles, but might not reflect current relevance or user preferences. LTR, trained on user search behavior, would learn to prioritize articles that users actually found helpful in resolving their issues, consistently providing the most satisfying and effective results.

The choice of ranking algorithm depends entirely on the specific needs of your cloud search system and the characteristics of your data. TF-IDF provides a simple and effective baseline. PageRank adds a measure of authority. LTR offers a powerful, customizable approach capable of superior performance, provided you have sufficient training data. Carefully consider your project requirements, available resources, and technical expertise to select the approach most suitable for your circumstances. Start with simpler methods and progressively explore more advanced ones as your needs and understanding evolve. Remember, iterating and experimenting is crucial. Continuous evaluation and refinement of your ranking strategy are vital for maintaining a high-quality user experience. The ultimate goal is to deliver relevant, timely, and accurate results to your users, always improving your ranking mechanism to better understand and meet user needs. Therefore, regularly monitoring and adapting your approach is fundamental to long-term success.

5.1 TF-IDF

TF-IDF, or Term Frequency-Inverse Document Frequency, is a fundamental algorithm in information retrieval. It's a statistical measure used to evaluate how important a word is to a document in a collection or corpus. Understanding its mechanics is crucial for building effective search systems, as it helps rank search results by relevance. At its core, TF-IDF quantifies the importance of a term within a single document and then scales this importance down relative to the entire corpus, giving more weight to terms unique to a specific document.

This weighting system is not just theoretical; it has practical applications in various search engines and recommender systems. For instance, imagine searching for "rare orchids" on a gardening website. TF-IDF would recognize that "rare" and "orchids" appear frequently in documents related to rare orchid species, thus boosting their ranking. Conversely, common words like "the" or "and" would have a much lower weight because of their prevalence across all documents. The beauty of TF-IDF lies in its simplicity and effectiveness in capturing the essence of document content. Its ability to sift through the noise of common words and highlight the truly important terms allows it to significantly improve search result accuracy.

Let's delve into the components of TF-IDF. The Term Frequency (TF) component measures how often a specific term appears in a particular document. A higher TF indicates that the term is highly relevant to that document. For example, a document discussing "cloud computing" multiple times would have a higher TF for "cloud" and "computing" than a document mentioning these terms only once or twice. This calculation is straightforward: count the occurrences of the term and divide it by the total number of words in the document. The result is a normalized score between 0 and 1, ensuring consistent comparisons across documents of varying lengths.

However, TF alone isn't sufficient for accurate ranking. A word that appears frequently in a single document might not be particularly useful for distinguishing that document from others. This is where Inverse Document Frequency (IDF) comes in. IDF measures how common or rare a term is across the entire corpus. Terms that appear in many documents are considered less distinctive and receive lower IDF scores, while terms that appear infrequently in a large number of documents have high IDF scores, indicating their potential to distinguish relevant documents. The IDF is calculated using the logarithm of the total number of documents divided by the number of documents containing the term. This logarithmic scaling helps to moderate the impact of very rare terms.

Combining TF and IDF gives us the TF-IDF score. This score provides a weighted measure of a term's importance, balancing its frequency within a document (TF) with its rarity across the entire collection (IDF). Documents with high TF-IDF scores for the query terms are considered more relevant and are ranked higher in the search results. The formula is simply the product of TF and IDF, yielding a single numerical value expressing each term's relevance to a particular document within the context of the whole corpus. Intuitively, a term with high TF and high IDF indicates high relevance.

It's important to note that implementing TF-IDF effectively requires careful consideration of preprocessing steps. Text must be cleaned, tokenized, and stemmed or lemmatized to ensure accurate term counting and avoid discrepancies due to variations in word forms. Stop words, such as articles and prepositions, are often removed to focus on the most informative terms. The choice of these steps significantly impacts the accuracy and precision of the final results, often necessitating adjustments according to the specific characteristics of the datasets being processed. The appropriate techniques will vary depending on the nature of the text data.

Beyond the core calculation, various weighting schemes and normalization techniques can further refine TF-IDF's accuracy. For example, sublinear TF scaling can help reduce the dominance of very frequent terms. Normalization of TF-IDF values helps to ensure that longer documents don't unfairly dominate the ranking. These refinements offer further opportunities for improvement based on the specific features of your dataset and the intended application of the search. The specific methods used can considerably impact final results. Careful experimentation and validation are essential for achieving optimal performance.

Implementing TF-IDF in a cloud-based search system involves several considerations. The scale of the data often necessitates distributed computing techniques, which demands careful orchestration of calculations across multiple nodes. Efficient data structures and algorithms must be utilized to handle the massive amount of text data while ensuring rapid query processing. Furthermore, indexing strategies need to be selected which maximize efficiency and data access for large scale datasets. These considerations are crucial for handling data volumes of a large scale in a scalable manner. Efficient data storage is a key requirement here.

Finally, remember that TF-IDF, while a powerful tool, is not a silver bullet. Its limitations include its inability to understand semantics or contextual nuances. It treats all words independently, failing to grasp relationships between words that may be crucial to semantic understanding. Sophisticated techniques, such as latent semantic analysis, might be more appropriate for applications demanding deeper semantic comprehension. Therefore, understanding its capabilities and limitations is crucial for selecting the right tool for a particular application. Always consider the specific needs and limitations before implementing this methodology.

5.2 PageRank

PageRank, at its core, measures the importance of a webpage within a vast network of interconnected sites. It's not simply about counting incoming links; it's about understanding the quality of those links. A link from a highly ranked, authoritative site carries significantly more weight than one from a newly created, low-traffic blog. This fundamental principle underpins Google's search algorithm and remains a cornerstone of relevance ranking in information retrieval. Think of it as a democratic vote of confidence among websites.

The algorithm itself is iterative. It begins by assigning each webpage an initial PageRank score, often equal for all. Then, it iteratively updates these scores based on the incoming links. Imagine the PageRank score as a pool of votes. A page receives votes from each page linking to it. However, the votes aren't equal; a page with a high PageRank distributes its votes more powerfully. This process continues until the scores converge, signifying a stable representation of relative importance.

Implementing PageRank in a large-scale cloud environment requires significant optimization. The sheer volume of webpages and links necessitates efficient data structures and distributed computing techniques. Consider a scenario involving billions of pages and trillions of links; storing and processing this information efficiently is a substantial computational challenge. To address this, techniques like graph partitioning and distributed matrix multiplication are crucial. These methods break down the massive computation into smaller, manageable sub-problems that can be processed in parallel across multiple machines.

Efficient storage is just as vital. We aren't just dealing with raw data; we need to store the graph structure representing the webpages and their interconnections, allowing for quick lookups and updates during the iterative ranking process. Database choices, such as graph databases or specialized distributed key-value stores, are essential for optimized performance in these situations. Careful consideration must be given to data partitioning strategies to ensure even distribution of the workload across the cluster and minimize bottlenecks. Beyond the core algorithm, practical considerations dominate implementation. Handling updates to the web graph efficiently is crucial. Webpages are constantly being created, updated, and removed. Strategies for incremental updates, rather than recalculating the entire PageRank from scratch each time, are necessary to maintain responsiveness and scalability. This often involves techniques that only recompute affected parts of the graph, minimizing computational resources and time consumed.

Furthermore, the PageRank algorithm's inherent limitations must be understood. It's susceptible to link spamming, where malicious actors attempt to artificially inflate their PageRank through unnatural link schemes. To mitigate this, sophisticated algorithms and techniques to detect and filter spam links are vital, incorporating various factors such as link context and anchor text analysis. These filters help prevent manipulation of the ranking process.

Finally, incorporating PageRank into a broader search system requires careful integration with other ranking signals. PageRank provides a valuable measure of authority and importance, but it's just one piece of the puzzle. Combining it with techniques like TF-IDF, which assesses the relevance of keywords within a document, and more advanced methods such as Learning to Rank, yields a more comprehensive and nuanced ranking system, thus providing the user with better search results. Ultimately, the goal is to present the most relevant and authoritative information to the user, and effectively leveraging PageRank is an integral part of achieving that goal in any scalable search solution. A thoughtfully implemented PageRank system can significantly enhance the accuracy and relevance of your cloud-based search engine.

5.3 Learning to Rank

Learning to Rank offers a powerful approach to enhancing search relevance beyond traditional methods like TF-IDF and PageRank. These older techniques, while valuable, often fall short when dealing with the complexity and nuances of modern search queries and user behavior. Learning to Rank, in contrast, uses machine learning to learn the optimal ranking function directly from data. This data, typically encompassing user interaction logs (clicks, dwell time, etc.), provides invaluable insights into what users consider "relevant." This data-driven approach allows the system to adapt and improve over time, continuously refining its ranking capabilities.

Unlike traditional ranking methods that rely on predefined formulas, Learning to Rank empowers the system to discover complex relationships between search queries, documents, and user preferences. For instance, a simple TF-IDF approach might prioritize documents containing many occurrences of the query keywords. However, a user's actual relevance judgment is often far more subtle and depends on factors beyond simple keyword matching—context, user intent, and even the current session are key considerations. Learning to Rank can capture these subtle nuances, ultimately delivering far superior search results.

The core principle behind Learning to Rank involves training a model on a labeled dataset of search queries and corresponding document rankings. This dataset represents the ground truth: the rankings that reflect ideal relevance judgments based on user interactions or expert assessments. Several machine learning approaches can be applied here, each with strengths and weaknesses. Pointwise methods treat ranking as a regression problem, predicting a relevance score for each document. Pairwise methods focus on comparing document pairs, learning which document is more relevant within a specific context. Listwise methods, the most sophisticated approach, consider the entire ranked list simultaneously, optimizing the overall ranking order.

Choosing the appropriate Learning to Rank algorithm depends on many factors, including the dataset size, computational resources, and desired level of accuracy. Some algorithms, such as gradient boosted decision trees, are known for their effectiveness and relative simplicity in implementation. Others, such as neural network-based models, offer the potential for greater accuracy but require more extensive training and computational power. Regardless of the chosen algorithm, careful feature engineering is crucial. Relevant features might include TF-IDF scores, query length, document length, presence of named entities, and various other metadata related to the content, query, and user context.

Implementing Learning to Rank requires a structured approach. First, gather and prepare a suitable dataset of user interactions. Data cleaning and preprocessing are vital to ensure data quality and accuracy. Next, select an appropriate machine learning algorithm and carefully engineer relevant features. Then, train the model using the prepared data, carefully monitoring its performance using metrics such as Normalized Discounted Cumulative Gain (NDCG) and Mean Average Precision (MAP). The model should be evaluated rigorously, possibly using a separate test set to avoid overfitting. The learned model is then integrated into the search system, replacing or supplementing existing ranking mechanisms.

After deployment, continuous monitoring and evaluation are paramount. User interaction data needs to be continuously collected and analyzed to identify areas for improvement and to retrain the model periodically. This ensures that the ranking algorithm remains effective in the face of evolving user behavior and changes in the document collection. Furthermore, A/B testing is crucial; Compare the performance of the system with and without the Learning to Rank component, to confirm the enhancement it is providing. Such continuous refinement is central to ensuring that the search engine delivers continuously improved relevance and user satisfaction. Finally, remember that integrating Learning to Rank is an iterative process. It requires ongoing effort to maintain and improve, reflecting the dynamic nature of user behavior and the data itself. Investing in this aspect ensures the longevity and effectiveness of your solution.

6 Monitoring and Optimization

Effective monitoring is paramount for any cloud-based search solution. Ignoring this crucial aspect can lead to degraded performance, frustrated users, and ultimately, project failure. Begin by identifying key performance indicators (KPIs). These metrics will vary depending on your specific application and architecture but should generally include query latency, throughput, indexing speed, and resource utilization (CPU, memory, disk I/O). Establish clear thresholds for each KPI, triggering alerts when performance dips below acceptable levels. This proactive approach enables swift identification and resolution of potential problems before they escalate. Remember that consistent monitoring is key.

Tools like dashboards and logging systems offer invaluable insights into your system's health. These provide real-time visualizations of key metrics, allowing for immediate detection of anomalies. Comprehensive logging, capturing events such as query execution times, indexing errors, and resource consumption patterns, is equally important. This detailed record provides a historical perspective, essential for identifying trends and pinpointing root causes of performance issues. Invest in robust monitoring solutions, capable of scaling with your system's growth. Don't underestimate the power of visualization; graphs and charts make identifying trends far easier than sifting through raw data.

System tuning involves optimizing various aspects of your search infrastructure to enhance performance. One important area is index optimization. Regularly analyze your indexes for fragmentation, outdated data, or inefficient structures. Strategies such as merging, splitting, and rebuilding indexes can significantly improve query performance. Another critical aspect is query optimization. Analyze query patterns to identify slow-performing queries, often caused by inefficient search strategies or poorly structured queries themselves. You might need to refine your query processing logic, optimize your indexing schema, or employ caching strategies. Carefully consider the trade-offs between these approaches.

Scalability is a crucial consideration for cloud-based search. As your data volume and user traffic grow, your system must adapt to handle increased load. A horizontal scaling approach, adding more servers to distribute the workload, is often the most effective. However, consider employing load balancing techniques to ensure even distribution of requests across all servers. Auto-scaling features, commonly available in cloud environments, automatically adjust resources based on real-time demand, minimizing downtime and optimizing resource utilization. Vertical scaling (increasing the resources of individual servers) can be a short-term solution, but horizontal scaling offers far greater flexibility and long-term sustainability.

Careful planning for scalability is not just about adding more servers; it's about architectural design. Consider using sharding techniques to partition your data across multiple indexes, improving query performance and reducing the load on individual servers. Implement robust caching mechanisms to store frequently accessed data in memory, reducing the need to access the underlying database. Don't forget the importance of testing your scaling strategies thoroughly before deploying them in a production environment. Simulate increased load conditions to ensure your system can handle the expected growth gracefully and prevent performance bottlenecks during periods of peak demand. Remember, scalability is not a one-time fix; it's an ongoing process of adaptation and refinement.

A critical component of optimization is efficient resource utilization. Cloud environments offer pay-as-you-go pricing models. While this flexibility is advantageous, it's crucial to manage resource consumption carefully to avoid unnecessary costs. Regularly monitor resource usage patterns to identify areas for optimization. This includes CPU, memory, disk I/O, and network bandwidth. Identify underutilized resources and adjust accordingly. Consider consolidating resources where possible. Automated resource management tools can help you optimize resource allocation and lower operational costs. Optimize your chosen database configuration and consider options like serverless architectures to further reduce costs.

Finally, continuous improvement is crucial. Regularly review your monitoring data, analyze trends, and identify areas for further optimization. Establish a feedback loop with your users to gather insights into their search experiences. Continuous monitoring, system tuning, and scalability strategies are not just technical exercises, but essential components of a successful cloud-based search solution. Remember, the goal is not just to build a system that works, but one that works efficiently and effectively, providing a positive user experience and a cost-effective solution. Optimization is an iterative process, requiring ongoing vigilance and adaptation to changing demands. The pursuit of optimized performance should be a core principle throughout the lifespan of your cloud search system.

6.1 Performance Metrics

Understanding performance in a cloud-based search system is crucial. It's not simply about speed; it encompasses a holistic view of efficiency, resource utilization, and user experience. We need to move beyond subjective assessments and embrace objective measurements to truly gauge success. Ignoring this vital aspect can lead to systems that are slow, unreliable, and ultimately, fail to meet user expectations. The subsequent sections will explore various metrics crucial for evaluating the effectiveness of your cloud-based search infrastructure.

Latency, the time taken for a query to return results, is a critical performance indicator directly impacting user experience. High latency results in frustrated users, and for many search applications, even fractions of a second can make a significant difference. Factors influencing latency include network conditions, database query speeds, and the complexity of the search itself. Regular monitoring of latency at different points in the system - from query submission to result display - is essential. Analyze these latency values to identify bottlenecks and make appropriate adjustments to improve response times. Consider distributed caching mechanisms or optimizing database queries to lower overall latency. Implementing performance monitoring tools that track and alert you to unusual latency spikes will provide crucial insights into potential problems. A well-defined Service Level Agreement (SLA) specifying acceptable latency thresholds will further contribute to effective performance management.

Throughput, measured as the number of queries processed per unit of time, reflects the system's ability to handle concurrent requests. A high throughput indicates a robust system capable of handling peak loads without significant performance degradation. This metric is directly linked to scalability, as a high-throughput system can typically scale more easily to accommodate increasing user demand. Improving throughput often involves optimizing query processing algorithms, enhancing database performance, and potentially scaling out your infrastructure by adding more resources. Monitoring throughput during peak hours and under simulated stress conditions provides valuable data for capacity planning and resource allocation. The ultimate goal is to maintain a high throughput while keeping latency low, a delicate balancing act requiring careful system design and ongoing optimization.

Resource utilization provides insights into how efficiently the system uses its allocated resources. Metrics such as CPU utilization, memory consumption, and disk I/O are key. High resource utilization might indicate a need for scaling up, while consistently low utilization suggests over-provisioning. Effective resource utilization directly translates into cost savings, as you pay only for the resources actually consumed. Regular monitoring of resource usage allows you to proactively identify potential issues and optimize resource allocation. Employing monitoring tools with detailed resource usage reporting and alerting capabilities is important for maintaining optimal performance and cost-effectiveness. Understanding resource usage patterns over time is essential for making informed decisions regarding scaling and resource management.

Error rates, encompassing all types of failures - from network errors to database exceptions, play a critical role. A high error rate significantly degrades the user experience, leading to lost productivity and potential data loss. This highlights the need for robust error handling and logging mechanisms throughout the system. Analyzing error logs helps pinpoint root causes and facilitates the development of more resilient systems. Moreover, tracking various types of errors separately—for instance, network errors versus database errors—allows for more targeted problem solving. Proactive measures such as implementing circuit breakers and retries can mitigate the impact of transient errors.

Finally, user satisfaction, though subjective, is a vital metric influenced by all the factors mentioned above. While difficult to quantify directly, feedback mechanisms - surveys, user reviews, and analytics of user behavior - provide invaluable insight. By analyzing user engagement metrics like bounce rates and time spent on the search results page, you gain a deeper understanding of how the system performs from a user perspective. Incorporating user feedback into the performance optimization process helps ensure that improvements directly address user needs. Continuous monitoring and improvement, guided by both objective and subjective metrics, ensure a highly effective and satisfying search experience. Remember, ultimately, the goal is not just a fast system, but a reliable, responsive, and user-friendly one.

6.2 System Tuning

System tuning is crucial for maintaining optimal performance in your cloud-based search infrastructure. Neglecting this aspect can lead to slow query response times, increased costs, and a degraded user experience. Think of it as regularly servicing a high-performance vehicle; consistent maintenance ensures peak performance and longevity. Effective tuning involves a multifaceted approach, beginning with a thorough understanding of your system's current state. This requires meticulous monitoring of key performance indicators (KPIs), such as query latency, throughput, resource utilization (CPU, memory, network I/O), and error rates. Identify bottlenecks by analyzing these metrics; a spike in CPU usage might indicate the need for more powerful virtual machines, while high network I/O could point towards inefficient data transfer.

Tools like cloud monitoring services (such as those offered by AWS, Azure, or GCP) provide invaluable insights into your system's behavior. These platforms offer pre-built dashboards and alerts, allowing you to proactively identify and address potential issues before they impact your users. Don't underestimate the power of proactive monitoring; catching problems early significantly reduces downtime and mitigates potential damage.

Once you've identified bottlenecks, you can begin implementing specific tuning strategies. For instance, increasing the number of index shards can distribute the load more evenly across your cluster, resulting in faster query processing times, especially with large datasets. This is particularly effective for applications experiencing high query loads during peak hours. Alternatively, optimizing your query itself might be necessary; carefully constructed queries, utilizing appropriate filters and aggregations, can significantly reduce processing time and resource consumption.

Furthermore, consider adjusting the heap size allocated to your search nodes. Insufficient heap size can lead to garbage collection pauses, affecting overall performance. Experiment with different heap sizes to find the optimal balance between performance and resource usage. This often requires careful experimentation and monitoring to determine the ideal value for your specific application and workload. Remember that over-allocating memory can also lead to waste.

Database tuning plays a pivotal role in overall system performance. For example, indexing strategies within your NoSQL database can significantly impact query speeds. Ensure you're using appropriate indexing techniques and regularly analyze query execution plans to identify areas for improvement. Regular optimization of database parameters and indexes is essential, especially in dynamic environments.

Beyond database tuning, consider the impact of network configuration. Network latency can significantly affect query response times, particularly in distributed environments. Optimizing your network infrastructure, possibly through the use of Content Delivery Networks (CDNs) for static content or optimizing internal network connections, can lead to substantial performance improvements. High bandwidth and low latency connections between nodes in your cluster are essential for optimal performance, especially when dealing with large datasets and complex queries.

Finally, remember that tuning is an iterative process. Continuously monitor your system's performance, adjust parameters as needed, and conduct regular load tests to simulate real-world conditions. Regular load testing allows you to identify vulnerabilities and weaknesses under pressure, enabling you to proactively address these issues before they become critical performance bottlenecks for your search application. By adopting this systematic and ongoing approach to system tuning, you can ensure your cloud-based search solution remains efficient, responsive, and cost-effective. This iterative refinement is key to the long-term success and stability of your search infrastructure. Consistent monitoring and optimization ensures your system continues to perform optimally as your data grows and user traffic increases.

6.3 Scalability Strategies

Scaling your cloud-based search solution isn't merely about throwing more hardware at the problem; it's about strategic planning and implementation. Understanding your growth trajectory is paramount. Will your data volume double annually? Will user queries increase exponentially? These projections directly influence your architectural choices and scaling strategies. Ignoring these crucial considerations can lead to bottlenecks, performance degradation, and ultimately, a suboptimal user experience. Precise forecasting, therefore, is the cornerstone of effective scalability.

Vertical scaling, or scaling up, involves increasing the resources of your existing servers, such as adding more RAM or CPU power. This approach is simpler to implement initially, but it has limitations. There's a practical limit to how much you can scale a single machine before it becomes inefficient or cost-prohibitive. Furthermore, a single point of failure remains a significant risk. Consider this approach for smaller-scale applications or as a temporary solution until you transition to more robust horizontal scaling.

Horizontal scaling, also known as scaling out, involves distributing your workload across multiple servers. This is the preferred strategy for handling significant growth and high traffic. By adding more machines to your cluster, you enhance overall capacity and resilience. The key here lies in leveraging load balancing to distribute incoming queries efficiently across the cluster. Redundancy built into the architecture ensures that if one server fails, others seamlessly take over its workload, maintaining service continuity and preventing disruptions to your users.

Data partitioning is a critical aspect of horizontal scaling. Instead of storing all your data on a single server, you distribute it across multiple nodes. Several strategies exist, each with its own strengths and weaknesses. Range-based partitioning divides the data based on a specific range of keys, while hash-based partitioning distributes data based on a hash function applied to the key. Choosing the right partitioning method depends on your data distribution and query patterns. Incorrect choices can significantly impact performance and scalability.

Choosing the right NoSQL database is vital for scalability. Different NoSQL databases offer varying levels of scalability and performance depending on your specific needs. Document databases excel at handling unstructured data, while graph databases are ideal for analyzing relationships between data points. Key-value stores offer high throughput and low latency, while wide-column stores are suitable for handling large volumes of sparse data. Careful consideration of your data model and query patterns is critical in selecting the optimal database to support your scalability goals.

Caching is another powerful tool in your scalability arsenal. By caching frequently accessed data in memory, you reduce the load on your database and improve response times. Various caching strategies exist, including in-memory caching, distributed caching, and content delivery networks (CDNs). Strategic implementation of caching can dramatically boost performance, especially under heavy load, providing a significant improvement in user experience without necessitating immediate infrastructural upgrades.

Regular monitoring is essential for proactive scalability management. Track key performance indicators (KPIs) such as query latency, CPU utilization, and memory consumption. Establish baselines for your KPIs and set up alerts to notify you of any anomalies. This allows you to identify potential bottlenecks before they impact your users. Proactive monitoring enables early intervention, preventing minor issues from escalating into major performance problems. Regular reviews of your scaling strategies are also crucial. Your needs may evolve as your application grows, necessitating adjustments to your architecture and scaling techniques. Adaptability is key to long-term success.

Finally, don't overlook the importance of automated scaling. Cloud platforms offer autoscaling capabilities that automatically adjust the resources allocated to your application based on demand. This eliminates the need for manual intervention, ensuring your system adapts seamlessly to fluctuating workloads. By leveraging these automated features, you can maintain optimal performance and cost efficiency while focusing on other crucial aspects of your application's development and improvement. Effective scaling is an iterative process, requiring constant monitoring, analysis, and adaptation. By following these strategies, you'll build a cloud-based search solution capable of handling substantial growth and providing a consistently excellent user experience.

7 Security and Privacy

Protecting your data and ensuring user privacy are paramount when building cloud-based search solutions. This chapter focuses on the practical implementation of robust security measures and privacy-preserving techniques. Neglecting these crucial aspects can lead to significant breaches, legal issues, and irreparable damage to your reputation. Consider this a critical component of your overall architecture, not an afterthought.

Implementing granular access control is the cornerstone of a secure search system. Instead of relying on broad permissions, you should design your system to allow only authorized users access to specific data sets. Role-based access control (RBAC) is a practical approach: define roles with specific permissions, and assign users to those roles. This allows you to manage permissions efficiently, particularly as your user base and data sets expand. For example, a data analyst might need read-only access to a subset of the data, while an administrator would possess broader permissions, including the ability to modify configurations and user access. Regular auditing of access logs is crucial to detect any unauthorized access attempts.

Data encryption, both in transit and at rest, forms another crucial layer of your security architecture. Encrypting data in transit protects against eavesdropping while it travels across networks, while encryption at rest safeguards the data when stored. Employ strong encryption algorithms such as AES-256 and utilize TLS/SSL protocols for secure communication. Consider implementing key management systems to safeguard encryption keys. These systems protect against unauthorized access to keys and facilitate secure rotation of keys to minimize risks. Remember, robust key management is just as crucial as the encryption itself; a compromised key negates all encryption efforts.

Compliance with relevant regulations and standards is not merely a suggestion; it is a legal requirement. Depending on your industry and the type of data you handle, you may need to comply with regulations like GDPR, HIPAA, or CCPA. Understanding these regulations requires careful study and diligent implementation. It's not enough to simply know the names of these laws. You need to deeply understand their implications for your search system and proactively build them into your architecture. This will involve data anonymization techniques, consent management mechanisms, and procedures for handling data subject requests. Failure to comply can result in severe penalties.

Beyond these essential measures, consider implementing regular security audits and penetration testing to identify potential vulnerabilities. A proactive approach is far superior to a reactive one. Regular reviews of your security practices should be conducted to address emerging threats and vulnerabilities, ensuring your system remains secure and up to date. This includes staying informed on the latest security best practices and promptly applying any relevant patches or updates. Think of security as an ongoing process, requiring consistent effort and attention.

Furthermore, you should design your system with privacy in mind from the very beginning. Privacy-enhancing technologies, like differential privacy and federated learning, can enable data analysis and model training without compromising individual privacy. These techniques often involve adding carefully calibrated noise to the data or performing computations on distributed data, preventing individual data points from being revealed. Think about data minimization - only collect and store the data absolutely necessary for your search functionality. Avoid collecting unnecessary personally identifiable information (PII), and consider employing techniques such as data masking to further protect sensitive data.

Finally, employee training plays a vital role in maintaining security and privacy. Educate your team on secure coding practices, phishing awareness, and appropriate handling of sensitive data. Regular training sessions, covering security policies and procedures, are essential to prevent human error, which is often a primary cause of data breaches. Implementing a strong security culture within your organization will improve your overall security posture. Remember, the strongest technical security measures are useless if your employees don't understand and adhere to security protocols. A proactive, well-trained workforce represents one of your strongest defenses.

7.1 Access Control

Robust access control is paramount for any cloud-based search system handling sensitive information. Think of it as the gatekeeper, diligently scrutinizing every request before granting access to your valuable data. Without a well-defined access control strategy, you risk unauthorized access, data breaches, and significant compliance violations. Implementing strong access control isn't just a security measure; it's a fundamental pillar of responsible data management.

A multi-layered approach is the most effective. First, consider granular user permissions. This means assigning specific access rights to individual users or groups, tailoring their capabilities based on their roles and responsibilities. Perhaps a data analyst needs read access to all documents, while an administrator requires both read and write permissions, and a guest user only gets limited read-only access to specific pre-approved documents. This granular control minimizes the risk of accidental or malicious data exposure.

Beyond simple read/write permissions, leverage role-based access control (RBAC). RBAC allows you to define roles, like "search administrator," "data curator," or "data analyst," each with a predefined set of permissions. Then, you assign users to these roles, streamlining the process of managing permissions for large teams. This efficiency is crucial, particularly in dynamic environments with frequent personnel changes. RBAC drastically reduces the administrative overhead associated with individual permission management, making it far more scalable and maintainable.

Cloud providers offer built-in access control services. Leverage these wherever possible. Services such as AWS IAM (Identity and Access Management) or Azure Active Directory offer robust functionalities for user authentication, authorization, and permission management. Integrating your search system with these services eliminates the need for building your own authentication and authorization infrastructure, significantly reducing development time and effort. Moreover, these established services are regularly updated with the latest security patches, ensuring your system remains protected against emerging threats.

Remember to regularly audit your access control policies. This isn't a one-time task but an ongoing process. Periodic audits identify any vulnerabilities or outdated permissions. Regular reviews ensure that your access control system remains aligned with your organization's evolving security needs and compliance requirements. Identify users with excessive permissions; revoke or restrict them as appropriate. Such proactive monitoring is key to maintaining a robust security posture.

Consider implementing multi-factor authentication (MFA) to further enhance security. MFA adds an extra layer of protection by requiring users to provide multiple forms of authentication, such as a password and a one-time code from a mobile app, before gaining access. This significantly reduces the risk of unauthorized access, even if credentials are compromised. While it requires a small investment in additional infrastructure, it's a worthwhile investment to protect your sensitive data.

Careful integration with your overall security infrastructure is crucial. Your cloud search system shouldn't exist in isolation. Align its access control policies with the broader organizational security policies and protocols. This ensures a consistent and unified approach to security across your entire IT landscape. By integrating seamlessly with your network security systems, firewalls, and intrusion detection systems, you can create a comprehensive security architecture.

Data encryption, discussed in the subsequent chapter, complements access control. While access control determines who can access data, encryption ensures that even if unauthorized access occurs, the data remains unreadable. These two are complimentary security measures, providing a robust defense against data breaches. They shouldn't be viewed as mutually exclusive; rather, they work synergistically to strengthen your overall security.

Finally, stay up-to-date with the latest security best practices and industry standards. The threat landscape is constantly evolving.

By regularly updating your access control policies and technologies, and staying abreast of emerging threats and vulnerabilities, you can ensure that your cloud search system remains resilient to the latest attacks. This continuous learning process is a critical aspect of maintaining a secure system. Regularly review compliance regulations and adjust your access control accordingly, guaranteeing you're continually meeting industry best practices and legal requirements.

7.2 Data Encryption

Data encryption is paramount in cloud-based search systems, protecting sensitive information from unauthorized access. Implementing robust encryption safeguards user data, maintaining confidentiality, and ensuring compliance with regulations like GDPR and HIPAA. Choosing the right encryption method depends on several factors, including the sensitivity of the data, performance requirements, and the overall security architecture of your system.

Symmetric encryption, utilizing a single key for both encryption and decryption, offers speed and efficiency, ideal for encrypting large volumes of data. However, secure key management is crucial; a compromised key compromises all encrypted data. Consider using robust key management systems, incorporating key rotation and access control to mitigate risks. Algorithms like AES (Advanced Encryption Standard) are widely used for their strong security and performance.

Asymmetric encryption, using separate public and private keys, enhances security by separating encryption and decryption keys. The public key can be widely distributed for encrypting data, while the private key, kept secret, is used for decryption. This method excels in secure communication and digital signatures, verifying data authenticity. RSA (Rivest-Shamir-Adleman) is a common asymmetric encryption algorithm, though computationally more intensive than symmetric methods. For optimal security, consider a hybrid approach, leveraging the strengths of both symmetric and asymmetric encryption. For example, use asymmetric encryption to securely exchange a symmetric key, then utilize the faster symmetric encryption for bulk data encryption.

Data encryption at rest protects data stored on servers and storage devices. This involves encrypting data before it's written to disk, ensuring its confidentiality even if the storage medium is compromised. Full disk encryption is a common approach, encrypting the entire storage device. File-level encryption, encrypting individual files, provides more granular control and flexibility. Cloud providers often offer encryption services, either managed or customer-managed, simplifying implementation. Carefully examine the provider's security and compliance certifications to ensure they meet your security requirements.

Data encryption in transit protects data while it's being transmitted over a network, such as during data transfers between servers or client-server communication. HTTPS (Hypertext Transfer Protocol Secure) is the standard protocol for secure web communication, utilizing TLS (Transport Layer Security) or SSL (Secure Sockets Layer) to encrypt data in transit. For other network communication, consider VPNs (Virtual Private Networks) to create secure tunnels, encrypting data as it travels over public networks. Regular security audits and penetration testing are essential to identify and address vulnerabilities in your encryption implementation. Staying updated with the latest security best practices and patching any discovered vulnerabilities is critical for maintaining a strong security posture.

The choice of encryption algorithms and key management strategies significantly impacts security and performance. Factor in your specific needs, such as data sensitivity, performance requirements, and compliance obligations, when selecting your encryption approach. Remember that security is not a one-time task; it's an ongoing process requiring continuous monitoring, updates, and adjustments to ensure the protection of your sensitive data. Consider integrating encryption into your overall data lifecycle management strategy, from data creation to disposal. This proactive approach reduces vulnerabilities and enhances overall security for your cloud-based search system. Remember, a layered security approach, incorporating multiple layers of protection, offers the most robust defense against various threats and attacks. Regularly review your encryption policies and procedures, adapting them to emerging threats and technological advancements to maintain the highest level of security for your valuable data. Ignoring security best practices can lead to significant data breaches, resulting in legal and financial repercussions, as well as reputational damage.

7.3 Compliance

Maintaining compliance in cloud-based search systems demands meticulous attention to detail and a proactive approach. Regulations like GDPR and HIPAA, along with industry best practices, dictate specific requirements that must be diligently integrated into your architecture and operational procedures. Failure to do so can lead to significant legal and reputational damage. Understanding these requirements isn't merely a box to tick; it's a continuous process demanding vigilance and adaptation as regulations evolve.

Data encryption, a cornerstone of compliance, requires careful consideration of both data at rest and data in transit. For data at rest, robust encryption algorithms like AES-256 should be employed, coupled with secure key management practices. Data in transit necessitates the use of secure protocols like HTTPS and TLS, ensuring data remains confidential throughout its journey across the network. The choice of encryption method should align with the sensitivity of the data and the specific regulatory requirements impacting your system. Remember, weak encryption is no encryption at all.

Access control is another critical aspect. Implementing role-based access control (RBAC) allows you to granularly manage user permissions, ensuring that only authorized individuals can access specific data or functionalities. This requires careful planning and regular audits to verify that permissions remain appropriate and aligned with your organizational security policies. Employing multi-factor authentication (MFA) adds an extra layer of security, significantly reducing the risk of unauthorized access. Consider implementing a least privilege access model, granting users only the minimum permissions necessary to perform their duties.

Beyond encryption and access control, regular audits and penetration testing are essential. These processes proactively identify vulnerabilities in your system and help you mitigate potential risks before they can be exploited. Choosing reputable third-party auditing firms can provide an independent assessment of your security posture, bolstering your compliance efforts and providing valuable insights for improvement. Regular security updates and patching are equally crucial, closing loopholes that malicious actors may exploit. A reactive approach is far more costly and potentially damaging than a proactive one.

Compliance extends beyond just technical measures. It requires robust documentation of your security policies and procedures, demonstrating to regulators and auditors your commitment to data protection. This documentation should clearly outline your data handling practices, access control mechanisms, incident response plan, and any other relevant security controls. Regularly reviewing and updating this documentation is vital to ensure its accuracy and reflects your current security practices. Maintaining a comprehensive audit trail is crucial for demonstrating accountability and tracing any potential security incidents. Proactive documentation isn't merely about compliance; it provides a clear roadmap for your team, facilitating consistent security practices.

Data residency and transfer are other critical considerations. Certain jurisdictions have strict regulations concerning where data can be stored and how it can be transferred across borders. Understanding and adhering to these regulations is essential to ensure compliance. This involves carefully selecting cloud providers who can meet the required data residency and transfer requirements, and implementing mechanisms to manage and track data movement. Ignoring this can lead to heavy penalties and reputational damage. Thoroughly investigate the data residency and transfer policies of your chosen cloud provider.

Finally, understanding the specific regulations impacting your industry is paramount. GDPR, HIPAA, CCPA - these are just a few examples of the many regulations that may apply depending on your organization's operations and the type of data you handle. Staying informed about these regulations and ensuring your system remains compliant is an ongoing responsibility. It's not a one-time task; continuous monitoring and adaptation are crucial for long-term compliance. Engage with legal professionals specializing in data privacy to ensure you are fully compliant with all applicable laws. Compliance isn't just about avoiding penalties; it's about building trust with your users and maintaining a secure and reliable search system. A truly compliant system reflects a commitment to data integrity and user privacy that extends far beyond meeting the minimum legal requirements. It builds a solid foundation for long-term success.

www.ingramcontent.com/pod-product-compliance
Lightning Source LLC
LaVergne TN
LVHW022021200926
848481LV00007B/2479
* 9 7 9 8 3 4 9 3 2 5 8 1 6 *